45498447R00068

Made in the USA
Lexington, KY
16 July 2019